LEAD
THE WAY

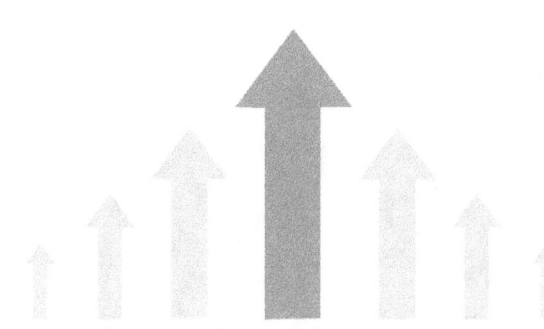

LEAD
THE WAY
A GUIDE FOR STUDENT LEADERS
Secondary School Edition

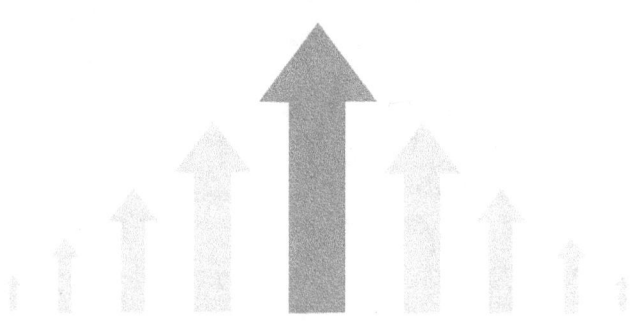

LUKE McKENNA

Copyright © 2025 by Luke McKenna

All rights reserved. Except as permitted under the Australian Copyright Act 1968, no part of the publication be reproduced, stored in a retrieval system, communicated or transmitted in any form or by any means - electronic, mechanical, photocopying, recording or otherwise without the prior written of the publisher.

Prepublication Data Services available on request from the National Library of Australia.

ISBN: 978-0-9943866-3-2

Edited by Rebecca Hood
Typesetting and Design by Mortuza Karzon

Published with the assistance of Lightning Source.

Contents

INTRODUCTION FOR STUDENT LEADERS 6

PART 1: PERSONAL SHIFTS 11

PERSONAL #1- FROM REACTIVE TO PROACTIVE 13

PERSONAL SHIFT #2- FROM BELOW THE LINE TO ABOVE THE LINE THINKING AND BEHAVIOUR 18

PERSONAL SHIFT #3- FOCUS ON YOUR CIRCLE OF INFLUENCE, NOT JUST YOUR CIRCLE OF CONCERN 24

PERSONAL SHIFT #4- FROM "HAVING" TO "BEING" 28

PERSONAL SHIFT #5- FROM PLAYING A SHORT GAME TO PLAYING A LONG GAME 31

PERSONAL SHIFT #6- FROM ORDINARY TO EXTRAORDINARY 33

PERSONAL SHIFT #7- FROM WORDS TO ACTIONS 37

PERSONAL SHIFT #8- FROM ENTITLEMENT TO GRATITUDE.................................... 41

PERSONAL SHIFT #9- FROM ME TO WE 44

PERSONAL SHIFT #10- FROM PAST AND PRESENT SELF TO FUTURE SELF 47

PERSONAL SHIFT #11- FROM FORCE TO STRENGTH 50

PART 2: LEADERSHIP SHIFTS.. 53

LEADERSHIFT #1- FROM BEING SERVED TO SERVING OTHERS 55

LEADERSHIFT #2- FROM POSITION AND POWER TO EXAMPLE AND INFLUENCE 58

LEADERSHIFT #3- FROM GOING UP TO GROWING UP: FROM PERKS TO PERSONAL GROWTH 62

LEADERSHIFT #4- FROM WIN/LOSE TO WIN/WIN 65

LEADERSHIFT #5- FROM DRAGGING OTHERS DOWN TO LIFTING OTHERS UP 68

LEADERSHIFT #6- FROM UNIFORMITY TO UNITY.. 71

LEADERSHIFT #7- FROM DOING WHAT YOU ENJOY TO DOING WHAT NEEDS TO BE DONE..74

BECOMING A LEADER WORTH FOLLOWING..76

CONCLUDING REMARKS: A VISION FOR TOMORROW'S LEADERS 79

ABOUT UNLEASHING PERSONAL POTENTIAL (UPP) 81

INTRODUCTION FOR STUDENT LEADERS

WHY READ THIS BOOK?

If you want to make a real difference—in your school, in your team, or in your own life—this book is for you. It will give you simple, powerful shifts you can start using right away to become a stronger, more positive leader.

These shifts aren't just about leading others—they're about learning to lead yourself first. When you put them into action, you'll find yourself making better choices, staying true to your values, and inspiring the people around you. Each shift is clear, practical, and designed to help you grow in confidence, character, and purpose. They're easy to understand, and when practiced every day can lead to real change.

You may have seen poor examples of leadership in the past, where leaders used their position for the wrong reasons, such as chasing popularity or trying to be the hero. That's not real leadership. Real leaders focus on making the lives of other people better, stay humble whilst doing so and do the right thing, even when no one's watching.

By reading this book, you'll learn how to become a leader worth following. A leader who people respect and trust.

WHO IS THIS FOR?

This book is written for secondary school student leaders—whether you've been given a badge or not. You might be a captain, a peer mentor, or someone who just wants to make your school and your relationships better. Being a leader isn't about wearing a badge and having a title; it's about how you show up and influence others. If you're willing to lead yourself well, this book will help you lead others with more confidence, purpose, and care.

We believe that school is more than just a place to get good grades. It's a training ground for life. The habits, choices, and shifts you make now will shape the kind of person and leader you'll become later. So, if you want your school, your friendships, and your community to be better—you need to make the shifts first.

WHERE DOES IT START?

It starts with you. Don't wait for the world to change. Don't wait for someone else to step up. If you want things to improve—at school, in your group, or even in your family—you need to take responsibility for your part. You have more power than you think.

> *"Never doubt that a small group of thoughtful committed individuals can change the world. In fact, it's the only thing that ever has."*
>
> *Margaret Mead*

Whether you're leading a team, a class project, a friend group, or just yourself—what you do matters. If you grow, others will grow too. When you stretch further, the people around you often stretch with you.

John Maxwell, a well-known leadership author, talks about the "law of the lid." This means that teams, groups and organisations can only grow as much as their leader grows. So, if you want to lead well, it starts with leading yourself well.

LEADERSHIP THAT LASTS

Some people want to be leaders for the wrong reasons—like gaining popularity or control. But real leaders don't focus on power. They focus on service. They care about helping others, making a difference, and growing a better community. And when they do that, their impact multiplies. Why? Because great leaders don't just add their effort—they inspire others to lead too. This is how strong school cultures are built—by leaders who grow other leaders.

WHAT DOES A "SHIFT" MEAN?

A shift means a small but meaningful change in direction. It's like turning slightly while flying a plane. Two planes might leave the same airport, but with just a small difference in direction, they can end up thousands of kilometres apart. Life is the same.

Your future isn't shaped by one big moment—it's shaped by small shifts you make every day: how you think, how you treat people, what you say yes to, and how you respond when things get tough.

Right now, you are where you are because of the shifts you've made so far. Where you'll be in five or ten years will be shaped by the next shifts you make.

At UPP (Unleashing Personal Potential), we run workshops for students to help them make these kinds of mindset shifts—to give them a new way of thinking and acting. Because if you don't know a better way, it's easy to keep doing what you've always done. But the moment you see a new way, you can choose it. That's the power of a shift.

CHOOSE YOUR PAIN: DISCIPLINE OR REGRET

One powerful idea that great leaders understand is this: in life, you can't avoid pain altogether. But you can choose between two types of pain—the pain of *discipline* or the pain of *regret*.

For example: Sleeping in feels great in the moment, but missing your commitments can leave you feeling regret later. Getting up early to get to sports training or music practice, or to study, or to help someone might feel tough in the moment—but that's the kind of pain that leads to strength, growth, and confidence.

Great leaders choose the pain of discipline more often. They know that good habits now create good outcomes later. They don't always feel motivated—but they stay committed.

LEADERS SHOW THE WAY

Great leaders don't just talk about the way—they show the way. They model it. They live it. That's why you need to make the shifts yourself first. Because you can't lead others to places, you're not willing to go yourself.

It's easy to understand this stuff—it's hard to live it. That's why leadership is rare. But if you commit to even one of the shifts in this book, you'll already be ahead of the pack. Because real leadership starts with small, consistent, personal change.

THE TWO PARTS OF THIS BOOK

Part 1: Personal Shifts – These are changes you make in your own thinking, actions, and mindset. You can't lead others until you lead yourself.

Part 2: Leadership Shifts – These are changes that help you grow your influence and effectiveness with others. If you're in a leadership position, these will take you from average to inspiring.

LEAD YOURSELF FIRST

If you don't lead yourself, people won't want to follow you. If you're always complaining, blaming others, or being unkind—why would anyone want to go where you're going?

The best leaders I've ever worked with weren't perfect. But they were growing. They were kind, thoughtful, and determined. They made small shifts in their thinking and actions every day. And people followed them—not because they had to, but because they wanted to.

That's what this book is about. Making small but powerful shifts that help you become a better human—and a leader worth following

PART 1: PERSONAL SHIFTS

Leading From the Inside Out

Before you can lead others well, you need to learn how to lead yourself. These personal shifts happen first because being a great leader starts with becoming a better person.

By working through the shifts in this part of the book, you'll grow as a person and develop the skills and character needed to lead others with confidence and care. When you make these changes, your life will improve, and you'll be able to better support, serve, and inspire the people around you—whether at school, at home, or in your community.

Here are the Personal Shifts we'll explore:

PERSONAL SHIFT #1 — From Reactive to Proactive
Take control of your choices instead of just reacting to what happens.

PERSONAL SHIFT #2 — From Below the Line to Above the Line
Move from negative thinking to a positive, responsible mindset.

PERSONAL SHIFT #3 — From Circle of Concern to Circle of Influence
Focus your energy on what you can actually change.

PERSONAL SHIFT #4 — From Having to Being
Become the kind of person who can achieve what they want.

PERSONAL SHIFT #5 — From Playing a Short Game to Playing a Long Game
Think beyond quick wins to long-term success.

PERSONAL SHIFT #6 — From Ordinary to Extraordinary
Choose to do your best in everything, even the little things.

PERSONAL SHIFT #7 — From Words to Actions
Make sure what you say matches what you do.

PERSONAL SHIFT #8 — From Entitlement to Gratitude
Shift from expecting things to appreciating what you have.

PERSONAL SHIFT #9 — From Me to We
Learn the power of teamwork and helping others succeed.

PERSONAL SHIFT #10 — From Past and Present Self to Future Self
Focus on growing into the person you want to become.

PERSONAL SHIFT #11 — From Force to Strength
Leading with true strength.

PERSONAL SHIFT #1-
From Reactive to Proactive

"Do you want to live by default or by design? The great thing is — you can choose. You are in charge."

Luke McKenna

Living by Default or Design?

Some people just drift along at school and in life — waiting to see what happens, letting things happen to them. That's called living by default. Other people make conscious decisions about who they want to be and how they want to lead. That's called living by **design**.

As a student leader, this is a key choice: Will you wait for things to happen, or will you help make them happen?

Great leaders don't sit back and react to everything. They're proactive — they make a difference by taking action, setting a positive example, and creating a vision for their group or school.

What Does It Mean to Be Proactive?

Proactive people write their own script.

They understand that their decisions, not their conditions, shape their lives.

"It's not about what happens to you, but how you respond to it that matters."

Epictetus

Whether it's a tough subject at school, a difficult conversation with a friend, or a team that's not working well together — proactive leaders don't just complain or wait for someone else to fix it. They stop, think, and choose how to respond.

Choosing to Choose

At every moment, you are faced with choices. The first and most important choice is this:

Will you choose to choose — or let others choose for you?

Some people avoid making decisions, and as a result, they give away their power. They wait, complain, or just go along with whatever is happening. Proactive student leaders take ownership of their decisions.

For example:

- o I can complain about group work... or I can step up and encourage the team to work together.
- o I can ignore a student who's being left out... or I can include them.
- o I can talk badly about someone... or I can encourage and support them.

It's not always easy — but even when it's hard, **you still have the power to choose** how you respond.

Thinking is Hard Work

Being proactive takes effort. It means slowing down and thinking before reacting. It means choosing your words and actions with care. That's why Henry Ford said:

> *"Thinking is the hardest work there is, which is probably the reason why so few engage in it."*

As a student leader, **are you prepared to think?** Are you ready to stop and respond instead of reacting without thinking?

What Happens When You're Reactive?

> *"Until we take responsibility for our lives, someone else runs our lives."*
>
> *Orrin Woodward*

Reactive people often feel like they have no control — like things just "happen" to them. They might say:

- o "There's nothing I can do."
- o "I have to do this."
- o "That's just the way I am."

When we say things like this, we give away our power. We assume the problem is "out there" — and we forget that we *still get to choose how we respond.*

You Are the Author of Your Own Future

"We each build our own future. We are architects of our own future."

Appius Claudius Caecus

"The best way to predict the future is to create it."

Abraham Lincoln

"All things are created twice."

Stephen Covey

Everything is created twice — first in your mind, and then through your actions. So, what future are you choosing to create?

Your Response = Your Power

Proactive people take responsibility — they don't pass blame or wait for someone else to act.

They develop what we can call:

RESPONSE-ABILITY — the ability to respond.

Too often we think:
Event = Outcome.
But that's not true.

The real formula is:
Event + Our Response = Outcome.

Imagine this situation:
A friend says something rude to you in front of others.

You could react by being rude back — and now there's an argument, or the friendship is hurt.

OR… you could pause, think, and respond with curiosity:
"Hey, that didn't sound like you — is something going on?"

Now, the friend has a chance to explain, and you might even become closer as a result. The difference was your **response**.

The **event** didn't change — your **choice** did.
That's the power of being proactive.

Being a Leader by Design

If you want to be a leader worth following, start by setting intentions every day. Decide:

- Who do I want to be today?
- What kind of leader do I want to be?
- What responses do I want to choose?

Living by design means **choosing your response** — and that choice is what gives you power.

Questions to Consider:

- Where in my life or leadership do I tend to react instead of respond?
- Where could I take more ownership or make a better choice next time?
- What's one small proactive decision I could make today?

PERSONAL SHIFT #2-

From Below the Line to Above the Line Thinking and Behaviour

↑↑↑

One of the most powerful mindsets shifts you can make as a student leader is this: You get to choose whether your behaviour is **below the line** or **above the line.**

Understanding the Line

Below the line, we live in what's called a victim mindset.
We fall into BED thinking:
- Blame
- Excuses
- Denial

This way of thinking is reactive. It makes us feel powerless and stuck.

Above the line, we switch to a victor mindset, where we own our choices.

We use OAR thinking:
- Ownership
- Accountability
- Responsibility

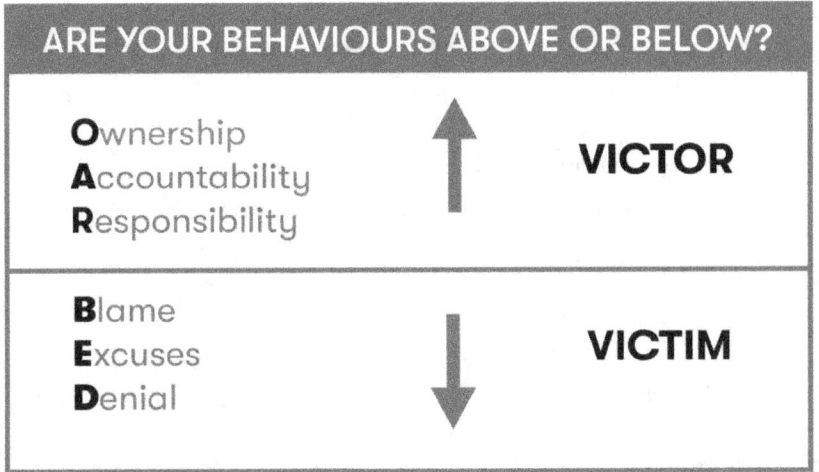

This is proactive. It's about stepping up, not stepping back. Its where real leadership starts.

Most People Don't Even Know They're Below the Line

Let's be honest — a lot of people operate below the line without even realising it. They complain. They make excuses. They say things like:

"It's not my fault."
"They should've told me."
"It's not fair."

But here's the thing: **blaming others never helps**. You can't control other people. You can only control how you choose to respond.

As author Christopher Pike put it:

> "Whenever we point a finger at someone else, we simultaneously point three fingers back at ourselves."

So, What Does Above the Line Look Like?

Let's say you mess up a project or forget to organise something for your leadership team. Do you:

- Blame someone else for not reminding you?
- Make an excuse about being busy?
- Deny it happened?

Or do you step up and say:

> *"That was on me. I forgot. I'll make sure it's sorted today."*

Taking ownership doesn't mean you're perfect. It means you're real, responsible, and ready to grow. And that's what leaders do.

Here are some examples of above the line and below the line thinking and behaviours.

ABOVE THE LINE
Thinking & Behaviours

- Accountable
- See Possibilities
- Ownership
- Seek & Provide Feedback
- Find Better Ways
- See It
- Look for Solutions
- Hope
- Take Action
- Make Choices

BELOW THE LINE
Thinking & Behaviours

- Excuses
- Deny
- Victim
- See Failure
- Find Fault
- Block Feedback
- No Control
- Blame
- Ignore
- Wait for Others

The Hard Part (and the Good Part)

Living above the line is harder in the moment — but it's so much more rewarding in the long run. Fixing the problem isn't always easy, but the process is simple:

1. See it.
2. Own it.
3. Solve it.
4. Do it.

It's easier to stay below the line. That's why many adults still live there! But that's not where student leaders belong.

The Window and the Mirror

At UPP, we talk about a leadership habit:

"Pass praise out the window, take responsibility in the mirror."

What does that mean?
- When things go well → Look out the window at others. Celebrate your team. Share the success.
- When things don't go well → Look in the mirror. Ask: "What could I have done better?" Learn from it. Take action.

Bad leaders do the opposite — they hog the credit and deflect the blame. Good leaders do what's right, not what's easy.

Choices Have Consequences

You are free to choose your response — to take ownership or to blame others.
But you're not free from the consequences of those choices.

- Break a school rule? There's a consequence.
- Cut corners on a project? People notice.
- Own your actions? You build trust.

- Put in effort? You get better results over time.

The choice is yours. But the outcome follows the choice.

Example 1: The Sam & Jordan Story

Two students — Sam and Jordan — both fail their science test.

Jordan uses **below the line thinking:**

"It's not my fault. The teacher didn't explain it well. The test was too hard. I'm just not a science person."

Jordan complains to friends, but doesn't change how they study. A term later, their marks haven't improved.

Sam chooses **above the line thinking:**

"I didn't do well, but I could have prepared better. I'm going to change that."

Sam asks the teacher for help, studies with a friend, and spends extra time on the hard topics. Sam still makes mistakes, but the effort pays off. By the next test, their results are much stronger.

Same starting point. Different mindsets. Different outcomes.

Example 2: The Alex & Taylor Story

Two players — Alex and Taylor — both get dropped from the starting line-up.

Taylor uses **below the line thinking:**

"It's not my fault. The coach just likes other players better. The ref never gives me a fair call. Training's boring anyway."

Taylor keeps going through the motions at training, doesn't work on skills, and stays on the bench for the rest of the season.

Alex chooses **above the line thinking:**

"I'm disappointed, but I need to earn my spot back."

Alex asks the coach for feedback, works on fitness, and practices after training. It's not instant, but the improvement is clear. Before long, Alex is back in the starting line-up and making an impact.

Same starting point. Different mindsets. Different outcomes.

One Last Thing

Above the line thinking doesn't just make you a better leader. It makes you a better human.

It takes courage. It takes self-awareness. But it leads to growth, impact, and respect.

Start with your next choice.

Questions to Consider:

- Where in your leadership or life do you tend to fall below the line?
- What's one area where you could take more ownership this week?
- Who in your life consistently models above the line behaviour?

PERSONAL SHIFT #3-
Focus on Your Circle of Influence, Not Just Your Circle of Concern

As a student leader, one of the most important things you can learn is this:

Focus your energy on what you can control, not what you can't.

This idea is all about understanding the difference between your **Circle of Concern** and your **Circle of Influence.**

Circle of Influence

Our circle of influence contains everything in our life that we can affect, change or impact through our actions. Examples include our behaviour, asking for feedback, our effort, our dedication to studying and learning and how we treat other people.

When you focus on these things, you grow as a leader—and your impact grows, too.

Circle of Concern

Our circle of concern includes the things which affect us, which we cannot control, influence or change. Examples of things in our circle of concern include how other people behave, the weather and how well the other team plays a game of sport.

Yes, these things can be annoying, frustrating, or disappointing—but they're not within your control. And focusing too much on them drains your energy and often leads to blame, stress, or excuses.

"If we try to control everything, and then worry about the things we can't control, we are setting ourselves up for a lifetime of misery and frustration."

Unknown

What I Can't Control
- Someone Else's Decisions
- How Others Treat Me
- Height
- Skin Color
- Death
- Others Taking Care of Themselves
- Who Likes Me
- Others Being Kind
- Who Loves Me
- Past Mistakes
- Others Being Honest
- If Someone Else Keeps Trying
- Others Forgiving Me
- Others Apologising to Me
- Weather
- Others Asking for Help

What I Can Control
- Doing my Homework
- Respecting Property
- Being Kind
- Being Accountable
- Studying for Tests
- The Friends I Choose to Have
- My Decisions
- Forgiving
- How I Respond to Challenges
- Trying Again
- How I Spend My Free Time
- Doing My Chores
- Taking Care of Myself
- Being Honest
- Asking for Help
- How I Respond to Other
- Apologising

What You Focus on Expands

This is a powerful truth in life and leadership.

If you focus on your Circle of Concern, it will take over your thinking.

You'll feel frustrated, like a victim, and powerless to change anything.

If you focus on your Circle of Influence, you become more proactive, capable and confident. You'll find that your circle starts to grow. People begin to trust you more. You learn faster. You become a stronger leader. That's because your choices, effort, and behaviour influence outcomes.

Let's say your soccer game gets cancelled because of rain. You can't control the weather (Circle of Concern), but you can use the time to work on your fitness or get ahead on your homework (Circle of Influence).

Another example: if someone in your class is being disruptive, you can't control their behaviour—but you can control your own focus, your own reaction, and maybe even be a role model to others.

Good leaders do this every day.

Proactive student leaders focus on their Circle of Influence.

Reactive student leaders get stuck in their Circle of Concern.

Shift Your Focus

Next time you're stuck in a cycle of complaining, blaming, or worrying, ask yourself:
- Can I control this?
- Is this something I can take action on?
- How can I respond as a leader?

If it's in your Circle of Concern, let it go.

If it's in your Circle of Influence, do something about it.

Questions to Consider:

- Where in your life are you spending too much time focused on things outside your control?
- How could you take action on something within your Circle of Influence this week?
- How can you model this mindset for others in your school or team?

PERSONAL SHIFT #4- From "Having" to "Being"

"You've got to be before you can do and do before you can have."

In short, you have to be a person of character and do the right things before you can have the things you really want.

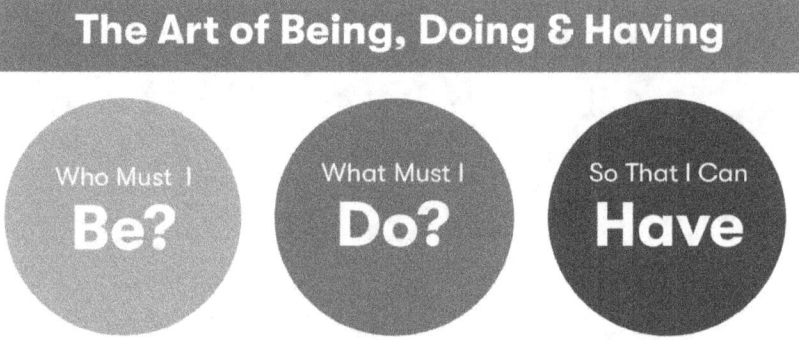

This idea is powerful for leaders. Often, we focus on what we want to have—great results, good grades, awesome friendships, or even recognition. But if we want to have these things, we first have to focus on who we need to be and what we need to do.

Let's break it down with the idea of Be → Do → Have. See some examples below:

Be → Do → Have		
Who Must I Be?	What Must I Do?	So That I Can Have...
Be organised	Study regularly	Good grades
Be a team player	Encourage others	A strong leadership team
Be respectful	Listen and include	Good friendships

To make this theory work in your own life, give this activity a go:

1. Start with the right-hand column. Write a few things you really want to have in your life. For example: great friendships, strong leadership skills, confidence, respect, or a spot on a school leadership team.

2. Next, move to the middle column. What do you need to do to make those things happen?

3. Finally, reflect on the left-hand column. What kind of person do you need to be to take those actions consistently?

Everyone wants to HAVE the good stuff.

Not everyone wants to DO the hard work or BE the person they need to be to earn those results.

Leadership coach Jim Rohn once said:

> *"The greatest reward to becoming a millionaire is not the amount of money you earn. It's the kind of person you have to become to be a millionaire in the first place."*

In other words, what matters most isn't achieving the goal—it's who you become while striving towards it.

Most people try to be happy or successful by focusing on what they want to have. But real leaders start with being. They grow their character, act with consistency, and then have the life and impact they want.

You can't put the cart before the horse.
It's always: **Be → Do → Have.**

Questions to Consider:

- How might you benefit by flipping your focus to being rather than having?

PERSONAL SHIFT #5-
From Playing a Short Game to Playing a Long Game

Are you focused on short-term rewards or long-term growth?

You may have heard the phrase:

> *"It takes ten years to become an overnight success."*

This reminds us that real success doesn't just happen suddenly. People who look like they've "made it" probably spent years working hard behind the scenes—making smart decisions, staying disciplined, and building their character.

As a student leader, it's tempting to chase quick wins—praise from others, awards, popularity, or a title. But true leaders focus on the **long game:** making daily choices that lead to lasting impact and excellence.

Practicing leadership skills, being kind when it's hard, showing up even when you're tired, studying without being told—none of those things are flashy. But they matter.

> *"Success is the sum of small efforts, repeated day in and day out."*
>
> *Robert Collier*

When you consistently do the right things—over weeks, months, and years—you get results that stick.

On the other hand, chasing quick results often means cutting corners, skipping growth, or doing what's popular instead of what's right. That might work for a little while, but it doesn't lead to true leadership or respect.

Here's a good reminder from a Chinese proverb:

> *"The best time to plant a tree was 20 years ago. The second-best time is now."*

So the best time to start playing the long game… is now.

Start becoming the kind of leader who keeps showing up. Who works hard even when no one is watching. Who makes decisions with the future in mind.

Because success and leadership never happen by accident. They are always the result of long-term thinking, daily action, and a commitment to growth.

Questions to Consider:

- What can you do each day to continue to improve yourself and prepare for long-term success?

PERSONAL SHIFT #6-
From Ordinary to Extraordinary

We all face a choice every day: Will we choose to be ordinary, or will we step up to be **extraordinary?** As a student leader, this choice becomes even more important — because your example matters.

Choosing extraordinary doesn't mean you're the best at everything. It means you consistently give your best effort. It means you do the small things with excellence — even when no one's watching.

Think about it. Some students just "cruise." They do enough to avoid trouble, but never enough to truly stand out. They settle for average — in effort, in attitude, and in how they treat others. That might be ordinary, but it won't make them memorable, respected, or impactful. And it definitely won't make them leaders others want to follow.

Excellence in the Ordinary

Leadership isn't about one big moment. It's about the small moments — the daily decisions to show up, to try again, to help someone else, to get uncomfortable, and to lead by example.

You don't need a spotlight to lead. True leadership happens when you:

- Listen when someone needs to talk.

- Speak kindly, even when you're tired.
- Keep your word.
- Own your mistakes.
- Bring a good attitude to your class, team, or group.

As student leaders, it's your responsibility to raise the bar — not just in what you do, but in how you do it. That's what it means to lead with excellence.

The All Blacks rugby team has a rule: No one leaves the locker room a mess — not even the best player. Why? Because how you do anything is how you do everything.

> *"Set your standards high, and keep them high, even if you think no one else is looking. Somebody out there will always notice, even if it's just you."*
>
> *Dianne Snedaker*

Strive for Better — Every Day

You don't become extraordinary overnight. Just like you don't get fit from one workout, or unwell from one sugary drink. Success comes from doing the small, ordinary things really well — over and over again.

That means:

- Saying yes to early mornings when it's easier to sleep in.
- Staying focused in class when it's tempting to scroll.
- Volunteering to help when others wait to be asked.
- Showing up with energy and purpose, even on hard days.

These habits shape who you are becoming — not just as a student, but as a leader and a person.

"Your success in your career will be in direct proportion to what you do after you've done what you are expected to do."
Brian Tracy

Going the Extra Mile

One of the most powerful habits of a great leader is going the extra mile. This means doing more than what's expected, and doing it with a great attitude.

- If you're asked to set up a room, you also tidy it afterward.
- If you lead an assembly, you also check in with others to make sure they're ready.
- If you're helping organise an event, you take time to thank the people who worked behind the scenes.

"The habit of going the extra mile... means rendering more service and better service than one is expected to render, and doing it with a positive mental attitude."

Napoleon Hill

Most people don't do this. That's why going the extra mile makes you stand out. It's why others will remember your leadership.

What Do You Want to Be Known For?

If you turn up late, unprepared, or with a bad attitude, people notice. And they'll start expecting that from you. But if you show up consistently with respect, preparation, and effort — they'll come to rely on you, trust you, and follow you.

That's leadership.

> *"Your thoughts become your words. Your words become your actions. Your actions become your habits. Your habits become your character, and your character determines your destiny."*
>
> *Lao Tzu*

As a student leader, this matters more than ever. You're not just representing yourself — you're representing your school, your peers, your values, and the future leader you're becoming.

So — what kind of leader do you want to be? And are your actions right now matching that vision?

Questions to Consider:

- How can I focus on excellence in the ordinary today — in my attitude, actions, and words?
- What's one way I can go the extra mile this week in my leadership role?
- Am I showing up in a way that reflects the leader I want to become?

PERSONAL SHIFT #7-
From Words to Actions

When someone says one thing and does another, which one do you believe?

It's easy to talk the talk. But leadership means walking the walk — doing what you say you'll do, and letting your actions speak louder than your words.

Aligning Our Words and Actions

Imagine a student leader telling others to respect each other — but then talking rudely to classmates or ignoring a teacher's instructions. What message does that send? At best, it creates confusion. At worst, it teaches others that saying the right thing is enough, even if your behaviour doesn't match.

When a leader (in a school, a team, or even a country) speaks about respect, honesty, or kindness — but acts differently — their credibility takes a hit. People stop listening. They stop trusting. They stop following.

As a student leader, your influence comes from the trust others have in you. That trust grows when your actions back up your words. If for some reason you need to go against something you've said or asked others to do, be honest and explain why. That transparency helps keep trust strong.

"No one wants to follow a fraud."

People tend to follow what they see — not just what they hear. This is because of something called mirror neurons in our brain. These neurons help us copy the behaviours of people around us — especially those we look up to. So, if you act with positivity, generosity and kindness, others are more likely to reflect those same qualities back to you.

If you show up with negativity, selfishness or judgement — don't be surprised when that's what you get from others.

You get back what you give out.

Values and Actions

In schools, you'll often see values written on the wall or in a handbook — things like Respect, Integrity, and Responsibility. But what do those values really mean?

Too often, people hope that words are enough. But they're not. Your values aren't something you hang on a wall — they're something you live out, every day.

Your real values show up in how you treat classmates, how you respond to challenges, and how you lead when things aren't going your way. You can't fake this stuff.

You may never say "I value honesty" — but people will know you do, because you're honest. You might never say "I value kindness" — but people will feel it, because of how you treat them.

"Values on the wall or webpage mean nothing. Values in action make a difference."

At UPP, our values are Character, Excellence and Contribution. We didn't just pick these words because they sound good. They came from how we were already living and working. We only gave them names five years after we started the program — but they had been part of our actions the whole time.

We've gotten better at expressing those values in words, but what matters most is that they are real to us. They guide how we speak, behave, and make decisions. They're not decorations.

They're the foundation.

I don't need to see values on the wall every day at work to remind me to live them. It's just how I am, or at least how I strive to be.

That's the key word: strive. No one is perfect — but a real leader keeps trying to live their values, even when it's hard.

When an organisation or school creates values based on who they want to be — not who they really are — it shows. People see through it. It's just talk. But when your actions are already aligned, putting your values into words becomes a powerful tool — not just to guide your own leadership, but to attract others who share those same values.

At UPP, clearly expressing our values has helped us find the right people to join us. People who don't connect with Character, Excellence and Contribution usually don't want to stick around — and that's a good thing. It means the right people are drawn in, and we can all challenge each other to keep growing into those values.

"If our values resonate with you, this is the best place to work. If they don't, it will be horrible — because we will always be challenging you on the values of Character, Excellence and Contribution."

As a student leader, this is true for you too. You set the tone. The values you choose to live by — not just say out loud — will shape the kind of leader you become, and the kind of legacy you leave behind.

Questions to Consider:

- What are your personal values that you strive to live by?
- Do your actions match those values — even when no one's watching?
- Are there certain values that you want to put into action more often?

PERSONAL SHIFT #8-
From Entitlement to Gratitude

Gratitude changes things

Great leaders show gratitude, not entitlement. They shift from complaining about problems to being responsible for finding solutions. They look for what they can do to improve a situation, rather than blaming others. They understand that while they're the centre of their own world, they're not the centre of the world.

Some people, on the other hand, are quick to complain. They're always looking for what's wrong. They expect things to go their way and feel annoyed when they don't. Instead of lifting others up, they tend to bring others down. The problem is—when you look for problems, you usually find them.

But there's a better way... you can train your brain.

Training your brain with gratitude

Over time, gratitude teaches our brain to scan our world and focus on the good. When we're looking for reasons to be thankful, we tend to find them. That's because of a part of the brain called the **reticular activating system (RAS)**—a kind of filter that helps us focus on what's important. Out of everything going on around us, the RAS lets in what we care about most, or what we're looking for.

So, if we look for positives—we're more likely to see them.

Psychologists call this predictive encoding—priming your brain to expect a positive outcome actually helps you notice it when it happens. Research shows that doing this makes us three times more likely to spot something good.

In the words of Henry David Thoreau:

> *"It's not what you look at that matters – it's what you see."*

The power of daily gratitude

Studies show that a daily gratitude practice leads to us feeling more alert, enthusiastic, determined, and energised. It's also linked to better sleep, more success at school, and stronger connections with family and friends (Emmons & McCullough 2003).

Grateful people also tend to bring joy to those around them. People enjoy being around someone who sees the best in life.

> *"He is a wise man who does not grieve for the things which he has not, but rejoices for those which he has."*
>
> *Epictetus*

> *"Give thanks in all circumstances."*
>
> *1 Thessalonians 5*

Being grateful helps wire your brain for more joy, more opportunity, and more positivity.

So… it's worth being a glass-half-full kind of person.

Question to Consider:

- How can I regularly practise being more grateful for the situations and people in my life?

PERSONAL SHIFT #9- From Me to We

Shawn Achor talks about **small potential** as the success we can achieve on our own, and **big potential** as the success we can achieve with others. Are you aiming to be a big potential or small potential kind of person?

Working well with other people is one of the best ways to achieve more. When we realise that other people have skills and experiences we don't, it makes sense to work together. You can go faster alone, but further together.

Some people like to go it alone, while others thrive in a team. But humans are social creatures — we're built to connect and collaborate.

The Wisdom of the Crowd

This idea shows that a group of diverse people often makes better decisions than one expert alone A famous example comes from a 1906 country fair in Plymouth, England. A contest asked 800 people to guess the weight of an ox. The guesses were all over the place, but when the average was taken, it was just 1% off the real weight. Together, we tend to make better decisions and achieve more.

You'll achieve more when you shift your focus from just me to we. When you focus on helping others, your own life improves as well.

Getting What You Want by Helping Others

It's simple: You can have everything you want — if you help enough people get what they want.

Be the first to give. Add value where you can. Support others. Sowing always comes before reaping. When you provide service and help others grow, great things tend to happen.

Rather than focusing only on ourselves, great leaders and great people shift to being **others-focused.**

When you do good work and help others, recognition and rewards usually follow. People are rewarded at the level they contribute. Make a bigger contribution, and you'll often see a bigger reward. But remember — the **contribution comes first,** not the reward.

As a young person, focus first on learning. Don't stress about earning just yet — that part will come later. If you **learn a lot, contribute a lot,** and **make a difference,** success will follow.

There are no shortcuts to making a real contribution.

In life, we first learn as students, then as doers, and then as leaders. But the truth is, we're always students. Our skills grow as we help more people. We learn more about ourselves and others through that journey.

Keep learning, keep contributing, and keep growing. Don't settle for where you are — always challenge yourself to grow and contribute more. The more you contribute, the more you grow.

The more you grow, the more you can lead.

My Shift

When I started UPP in 2015, I focused mostly on what I could do and how many students I could help. I realised I could work with about 10,000 students each year in person — that's my **small potential.**

But then I made a shift. I started focusing on helping our UPP team members succeed. Their wins became my wins. Their growth became my priority.

And that's when things really changed.

Now, our UPP team has helped more than 400,000 students since we began. Last year alone, we reached over 65,000 students. We hope to eventually support more than 80,000 Aussie students each year.

To do that, I have to grow — and help our team grow. I need to BE a better leader and DO the things that make that possible. Only then can we HAVE the kind of impact we want.

Want to do more? Help more people. Want to lead? Start by serving.

No matter what your future career or goals are, the best way to lead is to help others. The best way to grow is to shift from **me** to **we**.

Questions to Consider:

- How can you unlock more of your big potential?
- How can you offer more service, support, and help to others in your life?

PERSONAL SHIFT #10-
From Past and Present Self to Future Self

Your Future Self

"Always make your future bigger than your past."

Dan Sullivan

"Anyone who isn't embarrassed by who they were last year probably isn't learning enough."

Alain de Botton

In psychology, there's a concept called prospection. This means that the future you imagine for yourself is what drives how you behave right now. Whatever you see for your future shapes your actions today.

For example:

- If a student sees themselves as a school leader one day, they might start practicing communication skills or volunteering now.
- If someone wants to be a professional athlete, they will probably train hard and practice regularly.

If you don't imagine a bright or successful future for yourself, it's less likely you'll take steps to build one.

Why Your Future Self Matters

The way you think about your future self-determines how much effort and time you invest in yourself now. You don't need to have it all planned out perfectly — plans change! But having a clear and positive vision for your future helps you stay motivated.

Think about what kind of person you want to be in 3 years, 5 years, or even 10 years. How will you grow? What will you have achieved? How will you feel?

How to Build Your Future Self

One way to do this is by regularly reflecting on your progress and goals. Here are 5 questions you can write down every month to keep yourself focused and intentional:

1. Where am I right now?
2. What wins have I had in the last 30 days?
3. What are my goals for the next 30 days?
4. What do I want to achieve in the next 12 months?
5. Where do I want to be 3 years from now?

This helps you track how far you've come and where you want to go next.

Remember:

- Your future self is someone you create by the choices you make today.

- The better your vision for your future, the more motivated you'll be now.

Make Your Future Bigger Than Your Past

Always aim to grow and improve. Challenge yourself to be better every day, not just in school but also as a leader, friend, and person.

"The ability of the average person could be doubled, if the situation demanded it."

Will Durant

Questions to Consider:

- What kind of future do you see for yourself?
- What are you doing right now to move toward your best possible future self?

PERSONAL SHIFT #11- From Force to Strength

Have you ever noticed the difference between trying to push your way through something, versus moving forward with steady confidence and calm? That's the difference between force and strength.

Force vs Strength

Force is pushing, controlling, or trying to make things happen through pressure, anger, or frustration. It often causes resistance or conflict.

Strength comes from within—it's calm, confident, and connected to your values. Strength influences and inspires others without needing to push or control.

Why does this matter for student leaders?

When you lead with force, you might try to control others or push people to follow you. This can lead to stress, arguments, or people resisting your ideas.

But when you lead with strength, you:

- Show respect and understanding

- Inspire others by your example
- Build trust and cooperation
- Stay calm and positive even when things get tough

How to move from force to strength:

- Know your values and purpose. True strength comes from being clear about who you are and what you stand for as a leader.
- Control your emotions. Instead of reacting with anger or frustration, pause and respond thoughtfully.
- Listen to others. Strength grows when you respect others' ideas and feelings, even if you don't always agree.
- Lead by example. Your actions speak louder than words—show kindness, honesty, and commitment every day.
- Choose positive influence over control. Focus on inspiring others rather than forcing them to follow.

What this looks like in real life:

- Instead of yelling at your team when things go wrong, you calmly guide them to fix the problem.
- Instead of demanding respect, you earn it by treating others with respect.
- Instead of pushing people to do things your way, you invite collaboration and listen to new ideas.

Why shift to strength?

When you lead with strength, people want to follow you—not because they have to, but because they believe in you. You create a positive environment where everyone can grow and contribute.

Remember the idea that "strength gives; force takes."

Questions To Consider:

- Are you leading with force or strength? How can you tell?
- What small changes can you make today to lead with more strength and less force?
- How can you inspire others through calm confidence rather than control?

PART 2: LEADERSHIP SHIFTS

Becoming an Authentic Leader

There are a lot of different ideas about what leadership really means. Sometimes, when we think about leaders, we picture people who are rich, powerful, and always in control. They might seem strong and determined, but also self interested and lacking care for others.

Other times, we see leaders who are calm under pressure, kind, and focused on helping others. This can be confusing, especially when you're just starting out as a leader and trying to figure out what kind of leader you want to be.

Many people feel unsure about becoming leaders because they've seen bad examples—leaders who didn't treat people well or who made poor choices. That's why some schools and groups find it hard to find great leaders. And many talented people don't want to be leaders at all because they don't like the way leadership is often seen.

I believe this happens because a lot of people have the wrong idea about what leadership really is.

In this part of the book, you'll learn about some important Leadership Shifts — changes in the way we think about leadership. These shifts helped me become a better leader. At first, they changed how I thought. Then, as I put them into practice, I saw real changes in my life and leadership.

These Leader Shifts challenge common myths about leadership and help you grow into the kind of leader others want to follow.

Shifts That Bust the Myths About Leadership

LEADERSHIFT #1
From being served to serving others
True leaders don't expect to be waited on—they step up to help and support others.

LEADERSHIFT #2
From position and power to example and influence
Leadership isn't about the title or authority—it's about the example you set and the positive impact you have.

LEADERSHIFT #3
From going up to growing up
Leadership means being willing to give up some comforts or perks in order to grow and serve others.

LEADERSHIFT #4
From Win / Lose to Win / Win
Great leaders find solutions that help everyone succeed, not just themselves.

LEADERSHIFT #5
From dragging others down to lifting others up
Leadership is about encouraging, supporting, and building others up—not tearing them down.

LEADERSHIFT #6
From uniformity to unity
Leadership celebrates differences and brings people together, rather than forcing everyone to be the same.

LEADERSHIFT #7
From doing what you enjoy to doing what needs to be done
Leaders don't just follow what's easy or fun—they take responsibility for what needs to happen.

LEADERSHIFT #1- From Being Served to Serving Others

Leaders Lead by Serving

Being a leader doesn't mean people serve you — it means you serve your team. A great leader's job is to help their teammates grow, succeed, and feel supported. Leaders solve problems, carry some of the load, and make the team's work easier and better.

Serving Others Means Helping, Supporting, and Lifting People Up

Good leaders don't just boss people around. They listen, challenge, encourage, and share praise when the team does well. When problems come up, leaders use their experience to help fix them — making tough situations clearer and lighter for everyone.

Why Leaders Don't Expect to Be Served

Some people think being a leader means getting special treatment. But leaders who only ask for things without helping aren't respected or followed. Leaders give support, not just take it.

They stand with their team, especially when things get tough.

Filling the Water Bottles

When I was in high school, I was captain of my indoor soccer team. I thought being captain meant giving speeches and leading the team on the field. But my coach told me the most important job was filling the water bottles before every game.

At first, I thought, "Is that all?" But later, I realised that leaders serve in small ways too. Filling the water bottles means helping your team get ready and do their best — even if it's not the most glamorous task. Leaders make sure their team has what they need to succeed.

Why Do Captains Run Out First?

When you see captains run onto the field first, it's not just for show. They're leading their team by example — willing to do the hard work and face the challenge head-on. They get to practice early, stay late, encourage teammates, and take responsibility when things go wrong. Good captains are the first to step up and the last to give up.

Serving as a Leader in Your Life

Being a leader means serving your team and community every day — whether it's at school, in sports, or with friends. When someone makes a mistake, a great leader doesn't blame them but helps figure out how to fix it and learn from it. Leaders share the responsibility and help people grow stronger.

From Climbing Your Ladder to Building Ladders for Others

In life, we all climb our own "ladder" — learning new skills and growing ourselves. But real leaders don't just focus on climbing their own ladder. They help others climb theirs too by sharing what they know, coaching, and encouraging others to succeed.

These are the stages of leadership:

- **Ladder Finding** — Figuring out what you want to do and how to grow.
- **Ladder Climbing** — Building your skills and becoming good at what you do.
- **Ladder Holding** — Helping others start their climb by sharing knowledge and support.
- **Ladder Extending** — Supporting others to grow even more and take on bigger challenges.
- **Ladder Building** — Teaching and empowering others to lead and help others in turn.

Behind every success is a team of people supporting and coaching each other — each playing their role in ladder climbing, holding, extending, or building.

The best leaders focus on serving their team by holding, extending and building the ladder for others to climb.

Questions to Consider:

- Who are you filling the water bottles for today?
- Who can you help climb their ladder by holding, extending, or building it?

LEADERSHIFT #2-
From Position and Power to Example and Influence

Leadership isn't about the badge — it's about how you show up

A lot of people think that to be a leader, you need a special title, a badge, or a position like school captain, team captain, or club president. They believe leadership is all about being "the boss" or having power over others.

But the truth is, leadership is not about the title you have — it's about the influence you have on the people around you. Real leadership is about how you treat others, the example you set, and the way you inspire people to be their best.

My story: When a simple 'good morning' made a difference

When I was in Year 12, I was given the role of school captain. I got the badge, gave speeches, met important people, raised money and did all the official things. At the time, I thought that was what leadership was.

Years later, I was surprised to hear from a friend's younger brother that he thought I was a "really great guy." I asked what I'd done to earn that, expecting he'd say something about my speeches or the things I did as captain.

His brother told me that what really mattered was that every day, I said "good morning" to him with a smile — sometimes I was the only person outside his class who did.

That small, simple act made a bigger impact than any title or speech. It showed me that leadership is about the little things — respect, kindness, and showing you care. It doesn't require a title, a speech or a badge. And anyone can do that.

What does this teach us about leadership?

Leadership is about how you treat people and the example you set — not about how many people know your name or what badge you wear. Anyone can be a leader at any time by choosing to be kind, helpful, and respectful.

You don't need to wait for a special position to start leading. Every day offers chances to make a difference by how you act and treat others.

What is influence — and why does it matter?

Influence is your ability to affect how others think, feel, and act. When you're a positive influence, you inspire people to do better and be better — even without telling them what to do.

For student leaders, influence might look like:

- Following school or classroom rules, encouraging others to do the same
- Inviting someone who's alone to join a game or group at lunchtime

- Helping a new student find their way around school
- Speaking up and being upstanding when you see unfairness or bullying
- Working hard in class and encouraging others to keep trying

These are all ways you lead by example and influence others in a positive way.

How do you build influence as a leader?

You build influence by showing up consistently as someone others can trust and respect. This means living the personal shifts you've learned, like being responsible, proactive, and respectful every day.

At UPP, we use the ASPIRE framework to help students grow as leaders:

- *ACTION:* Take the first step, and do what needs to be done without waiting
- *SERVICE:* Help others because you want to, not just to get something back
- *PERSISTENCE:* Keep going even when things get tough
- *INFLUENCE:* Use your actions and words to positively impact others
- *RESPECT:* Treat everyone fairly, even when it's hard
- *ENCOURAGEMENT:* Support and cheer on those around you

Living these values helps you naturally build influence — people will listen to and follow you because they see that you care and act with integrity.

What real leaders look like

Real leaders are often not the loudest or flashiest people. Sometimes they're quiet and humble. What makes them leaders is their kindness, courage, fairness, and willingness to step up when it matters.

They don't wait to be asked; they look for ways to help and improve their team or community.

They don't lead for praise or power — they lead because they care deeply about the people and goals they believe in. People follow these leaders because they trust them — they know that their leader will do the right thing and stand with them, especially when things get tough.

Why this matters for you

You might not be the school captain or hold a formal leadership role right now. But that doesn't mean you can't be a leader. Leadership is something anyone can practice — every day, in small ways — by how you treat others and the example you set.

Start by asking yourself:

How can I build my influence for the good of others through my actions and relationships today?

What's one small thing you can do this week to show kindness, take responsibility, or support someone else? Remember, real leadership is earned through respect and example — not a badge or title.

Questions to Consider:

- How can I build my influence for the good of others through my teamwork, relationships or role?
- How can I use the ASPIRE framework to set a good example when working with others?

LEADERSHIFT #3-
From Going Up to Growing Up

The Perks — What leadership looks like on the surface

Many people think leaders get the coolest perks — special titles, extra privileges, or recognition. At school, captains and prefects might have badges, more responsibilities, or some freedoms others don't.

It's easy to want these perks. Who wouldn't want to stand out? But real leadership isn't just about collecting rewards — it's about growing up and becoming someone others can trust and follow.

Growing Up — What leadership really means

Leadership means growing up — learning new skills, becoming more responsible, and building your character. It means:

- Showing up early and staying late when your team needs you
- Developing the courage to speak up for what's right, even when it's hard
- Learning to listen carefully and understand others' feelings
- Taking responsibility when things don't go well, and helping find solutions

- Being patient, kind, and consistent, even when no one's watching

Growing up as a leader means you don't just want perks — you want to be the best person you can be for your team and community.

Why this matters?

Some people want leadership for the perks but aren't ready to grow. That kind of leadership won't last because teams need leaders who show maturity, skill, and care.

Good leaders focus on growing themselves — in skills, character, and understanding — so they can support and inspire others.

My story: Moving from "What can I get?" to "How can I grow?"

Early in my leadership journey, I focused on what I could get — the titles, the recognition, the rewards. But I soon realised leadership is really about growing up: becoming a stronger, wiser, kinder person who can help others succeed.

Now, my goal is to keep growing — learning, listening, supporting, and improving — so I can lead by example and help my team grow too.

What this means for you as a student leader

You might not have all the perks yet, but leadership gives you the chance to grow — to develop new skills, confidence, and maturity.

That could mean:

- Practicing teamwork and communication so you can support your group better
- Taking on challenges even if they're uncomfortable
- Being a role model by doing what's right, not just what's easy

- Helping others feel included and valued
- Learning from mistakes and encouraging your team to do the same

The earlier you start focusing on growing up as a leader, the stronger and more respected you'll become.

Questions to Consider:

- How am I growing as a leader and person?
- What new skills or habits can I develop to support my team better?
- What is one way I can show more responsibility or maturity this week?

LEADERSHIFT #4-
From Win/Lose to Win/Win

What does "win-win" mean?

Sometimes people think that for one person or team to win, someone else has to lose. Maybe you've seen it in sports, games, or even at school — if one team scores, the other loses. But real leadership looks for ways where everyone can win together.

This is called win-win — when two or more people or groups find solutions that help all of them succeed.

The Power of Working Together: Mutualism

In nature, some animals have special partnerships where both benefit. For example, a fish and a shrimp work as a team: the shrimp digs a safe home in the sand where both live, and the fish warns the shrimp of danger. Both get something important, so they both win.

We can do the same in our relationships and teams. When we work together, help each other, and look for solutions that benefit everyone, the whole group becomes stronger.

Win-Win or No Deal

At school, this could mean finding ways for everyone to share success. Maybe your group is working on a project — instead of competing to be the only one praised, you focus on making sure everyone learns and contributes.

Here's a real example in the context of UPP. When schools need help, UPP provides workshops. The school wins by getting what it needs, the students win by learning new skills, the UPP team members win because they enjoy their work and get paid. Everyone benefits — that's a win-win-win!

In everyday life, think about going to a shop. The customer wins by getting what they want, the store wins by making money, and the workers win by having a job. Everyone's better off when all sides benefit.

Why Win-Win Matters for You

If a friendship, team, or group only benefits one person, it's not fair or lasting. Good leaders help find solutions where everyone gains something valuable.

If a deal or decision doesn't work for everyone, it's better to say "no deal" — meaning it's better to wait or find another way than force a solution where someone loses.

The Importance of Giving

A big part of win-win is learning to give — your time, your help, your kindness — without expecting something back right away.

At UPP, we have a challenge called #ItsGoodToGive — where team members buy coffee or treats for others just to spread kindness. Giving feels good and often leads to more good coming back.

For example, during a tough time like COVID-19 lockdown, my family received a surprise delivery of food and toys from a friend. That kindness made a hard time easier, and it reminds us that giving to others creates strong connections.

What Can You Do?

Look for ways to create win-win moments in your school, sports team, or friendship group. Think about:

- How can you help others get what they need while also reaching your goals?
- What can you give to support your teammates, classmates, or friends?
- How can you solve problems so everyone feels like a winner?

Leaders don't compete to win alone — they lead so everyone wins.

Question to Consider:

- Where can you find or create more win-win situations in your life?

LEADERSHIFT #5-
From Dragging Others Down to Lifting Others Up

"Strong people don't put others down. They lift them up."

Michael P. Watson

How do you react when someone else succeeds?

When someone in your class, team, or group does something great, how do you feel? Do you feel happy for them, or do you feel a little jealous or worried? Sometimes, when people feel unsure about themselves, they might try to put others down to feel better. But that doesn't help anyone — it only makes things worse.

Remember: someone else's success doesn't take away from your chances to succeed. And putting others down won't make you better or stronger.

Why lifting others up matters

There's a famous saying by Robert Ingersoll: "We rise by lifting others." This means that when you help others succeed and feel good about themselves, you also become stronger as a person and as a leader. Think about it like this: if a rising tide lifts all the boats in the harbour, when you lift someone else up, it lifts everyone — including you.

Real teamwork is about support

A few years ago, I was talking with some leaders in our team. We were thinking about who might be ready for a new challenge or responsibility. Instead of competing against each other, two team members actually spoke highly of each other — they lifted each other up with respect and support.

That's what real leaders do. They cheer on others and help their teammates grow.

Why giving compliments is powerful

You might notice that when you give someone a genuine compliment or say "great job," it feels good for both of you. Compliments show that you notice and appreciate the good in others — and that makes people want to support you back.

Good leaders are generous with praise. They don't just criticise or compete — they encourage and build others up.

Your challenge for today:

Can you find two people to give a real compliment to? It could be a teammate, a classmate, or someone you know. Say something kind and specific — like "I really liked how you helped out in class today" or "You did a great job in that game!"

Great leaders build others up — and when you do, you all rise together.

Question to Consider:

- Who can you lift up today?
- How can you help others feel stronger and more confident?

LEADERSHIFT #6-
From Uniformity to Unity

Why sameness isn't the goal

Sometimes, people think leaders should only work with people who are just like them — who think the same way or act the same. But great leaders know that's a mistake. Good leaders actually look for people who have different skills and ideas, because those differences make the whole team stronger.

Different types of leaders bring different strengths

In our leadership workshops, we talk about three kinds of leaders — and everyone is a mix of these, but some people are stronger in one area than others:

- **Prophet leaders:**

These leaders are full of ideas. They love to brainstorm and dream about new possibilities. They are creative and excited about the future, and their ideas inspire others. They're the "light bulb" people who spark innovation.

- **Planner leaders:**

These leaders are the organisers. They focus on the details, make plans, create schedules, and get things done. They think about who needs to do what, when, and how. They love ticking off tasks and making sure things run smoothly.

- **People leaders:**

These leaders care deeply about others. They listen well, support people, and help make sure everyone feels included. They build strong friendships and encourage their teammates. People tend to follow them because of the trust they build.

Everyone brings something important

No one is perfect or has all these skills — not even the best leaders. The smartest leaders know their own strengths and also know when to ask others for help. By doing this, they help other people grow and make the whole team better.

What does this look like in real life?

Imagine you and your friends are planning a fundraiser for a cause you care about.

- The prophet leaders come up with ideas for the fundraiser. Maybe it's a bake sale, a sports event, or a talent show.
- The planner leaders work out the details — where it will be, what you need to do, when everything will happen, and who will help.
- The people leaders make sure everyone on the team knows their role, feels included, and is excited to be part of the event.

All three types of leadership are needed to make the fundraiser a success.

Why this matters to you

Sometimes, you might be tempted to only listen to people who think like you or agree with you.

But when you appreciate and use the different strengths of everyone around you, your team can achieve much more.

For example, at UPP, our team members have different strengths and think about things differently — but because we listen to each other, we make better decisions and help more people.

It's the same in school clubs, sports teams, or student councils. When leaders don't listen to others, they risk missing important ideas and losing the support of their team.

Great leadership isn't about everyone being the same. It's about **working together, celebrating differences, and uniting strengths** to make something amazing happen.

Questions to Consider:

- What kind of leader are you most like — a prophet, planner, or people leader?
- How can you bring out the best in the different strengths of your friends and teammates to help your whole group succeed?

LEADERSHIFT #7-
From Doing What You Enjoy to Doing What Needs to Be Done

Doing what you like vs. stepping up for the team

It's natural to want to do the things you enjoy and feel good at. When you focus on what you like, you usually do that part well. That's how good workers or team members act — they use their strengths and get things done.

But great leaders — the ones who really make a difference — don't just stick to what's fun or easy for them. They look at what the whole team, group, or school needs, and they step up to do those things — even if they're tough or not enjoyable.

Going above and beyond

Great leaders don't just do the minimum. They do a little more. They help solve problems before someone asks. They take initiative — which means they start doing something important without waiting for instructions. But they do this in a respectful way, making sure they don't get in the way of others.

Sometimes, doing what needs to be done means doing things others avoid. That's part of being a leader — being the first to do the hard or unpopular jobs.

Real example: The All Blacks and "sweeping the sheds"

In his book Legacy, James Kerr shares a story about the All Blacks, New Zealand's famous rugby team. They are one of the best teams in the world, with lots of superstars and championships.

But here's the interesting part: after every game, the players themselves clean up the locker room. They sweep the floor, throw away trash, and tidy up. And it's not the newest or least experienced players who do this — it's the senior players, the team's leaders.

Even though they have big contracts and are super important, they don't think any job is too small or beneath them. If something needs to be done, the real leaders do it.

What this means for you

If you want to grow as a leader — in your family, your school, or any group you belong to — look for the things that need doing. Step up and do those things. When everything is going well, be humble and share credit with your team.

This is what makes a leader stand out: focusing on the needs of others and the team, not just on what's easiest or most fun.

Question to Consider:

- Where can I add value by focusing on what needs to be done — even if it's not what I enjoy — for the good of my family, school, or community?

Becoming a Leader Worth Following

Leadership Is About Influence, Not Position

True leadership doesn't come from a title, badge, or position. It comes from influence — the ability to make a positive impact on others through respect, kindness, and example. You don't need to wait for a leadership role to start leading. Every day, in small ways, you can influence those around you and make a difference.

Leadership Requires Growth and Responsibility

Leadership isn't always easy or fun. It's about growing up—developing your skills, character, and courage to do what's right, even when it's difficult. Real leaders do what needs to be done, not just what they enjoy. They take responsibility for their actions and for supporting the people around them.

Leadership Means Lifting Others Up

Great leaders don't put others down to feel better about themselves. Instead, they lift others up by encouraging, praising, and helping them succeed. When you support and celebrate others, you build a stronger team and community—and you grow as a leader yourself.

Leadership Thrives on Unity and Diversity

No one person can do it all. Leadership works best when you embrace different skills and ideas. Some leaders are creative thinkers, others are planners, and some are great with people. Together, these strengths create unity and help a team succeed. Celebrate the unique talents of those around you and learn to work with people who think differently.

Leadership Is About Giving, Not Getting

At first, leadership might seem like a way to get perks or recognition. But the best leaders realise it's about giving to others—giving your time, energy, and talents to help the group succeed. When you focus on what you can give instead of what you can get, you create lasting value and earn real respect.

Leadership Means Seeking Win-Win Outcomes

Leadership isn't about winning at someone else's expense. It's about finding ways where everyone benefits together. Whether in teamwork, school projects, or friendships, look for solutions that help everyone succeed. This attitude builds trust and lasting relationships.

Leadership Requires Authentic Roles and Actions

Leadership isn't just about having a badge or a title. It's about having real responsibility and making a genuine contribution. Avoid "tokenistic" leadership—where titles don't mean much—and aim for roles where you can serve, act, and make a difference for your school and community.

You Are a Leader Right Now

Whether or not you have a formal title, you have the power to lead every day. Leadership is shown in how you treat others, how you handle challenges, and how you step up when needed. Start where you are, with what you have, and commit to becoming the kind of leader others want to follow.

Leadership is a journey of growth, service, and connection. It's about learning to influence positively, lift others, embrace differences, give generously, and seek the best for everyone.

Keep practicing these shifts in your daily life, and you will become a leader worth following—not just at school, but for life.

Concluding Remarks: A Vision for Tomorrow's Leaders

I have a dream — that every student, especially student leaders, will experience leadership in a way that shapes not only their skills but also their mindset for life. Leadership is more than just tasks or titles. It's about embracing new ways of thinking and acting that can change your school, community, and the world for the better.

Imagine this:

Twenty years from now, business, government, education, healthcare, media, and beyond, will need leaders who care deeply for their people and their planet. Leaders who focus on serving others, not being served. Leaders who look for win-win solutions instead of thinking someone has to lose for them to win. Leaders who take responsibility for helping solve the big problems our world faces.

Albert Einstein once said,

> *"We cannot solve our problems with the same thinking we used when we created them."*

This means we need new ways of leading—leaders who think differently, act with courage, and care deeply.

Michael Fullan and Mary Jean Gallagher, in their book The Devil is in the Details, warn us that humanity is at a critical tipping point. The gap between the privileged and the disadvantaged is growing. People often focus too much on status and themselves, making it harder to come together. What we need is a **new moral purpose: to become better learners, better leaders, and better people.**

For the world to thrive, students must develop into leaders who:

- Are trustworthy, respectful, and principled
- Care for people, the environment, and global goals like the UN's Sustainable Development Goals
- Take positive action to serve others
- Seek to unite, not divide
- Focus on contributing rather than taking
- Are mentally strong enough to face complex challenges
- Lift others up instead of putting them down

These skills and attitudes don't come automatically—they must be learned and practiced. This book aims to help you become aware of these shifts—both in how you think about yourself and how you lead others. By embracing these personal and leadership changes, you will not only become a better leader but also a better human being—and together, we can make the world a better place.

About Unleashing Personal Potential (UPP)

At UPP, our mission is simple: to help every student become the best they can be. We aim to impact thousands of students every year, helping them learn, live, and lead better through workshops, camps, and teacher training. Since 2015, we've reached over 400,000 students across Australia, inspiring them to grow in character, excellence, and contribution.

About the Author

Luke McKenna, founder of UPP, is an educator passionate about helping students and schools unlock their potential. With experience as a teacher, school leader, and educational author, Luke has worked across Australia supporting young people to thrive. He holds degrees in Business and Education, a Master's in Educational Leadership, and a certificate in Positive Education. Luke lives in Brisbane with his wife Laura and their three children, and continues to speak and write about leadership and wellbeing.

A Note of Gratitude

After years of this journey, I am deeply grateful—to the inspiring educators I've worked alongside, to the passionate team who make this work possible, and most of all to my family, who support and encourage me every day. It is an honor to share this leadership journey with you.

Lead with heart, lead with courage, and always choose to lift others as you rise.

Your leadership journey starts now.

www.ingramcontent.com/pod-product-compliance
Lightning Source LLC
Chambersburg PA
CBHW050330010526
44119CB00050B/738